Exploration
&
Discovery

Exploration
&
Discovery

The Chronicle of American History
from 1492 to 1606

973
EXP

A Bluewood Book

This edition produced and published in 1996 by Bluewood Books,
a division of The Siyeh Group, Inc.
P.O. Box 460313,
San Francisco, CA 94146.

ISBN 0-912517-19-0

Printed in USA

Designed and Edited by Bill Yenne

Also in the *Making of America* Series:
Our Colonial Period (1607-1770)

Other titles of interest from
Bluewood Books:

100 Events That Shaped World History
100 Inventions That Shaped World History
100 Women Who Shaped World History
100 Men Who Shaped World History
100 Athletes Who Shaped Sports History
100 Folk Heroes Who Shaped World History
100 African-Americans Who Shaped American History
100 Great Cities of World History
100 Natural Wonders of the World

TABLE OF CONTENTS

THE
GREAT DISCOVERY

The pivotal event in American history occurred on October 12, 1492. It was then that an Italian ship captain, flying under a Spanish flag, set foot on the Caribbean island of San Salvador and congratulated himself on reaching Asia.

Until well into the twentieth century, this moment was proudly identified as "the Discovery of America." It was not literally the discovery of America, nor was it the first discovery of the American land mass by Europeans. America was "discovered" by the ancestors of Native Americans 25,000 years before, and it was generally known as early as the nineteenth century that other Europeans had camped on American shores 500 years before the Italian navigator raised his Spanish flag on San Salvador.

Why then is 1492 such a pivotal date? It is because from this moment, the tide of exploration would not stop, and the two hemispheres were inextricably linked.

At the time that Christopher Columbus (1451-1506) first set foot in the Americas, there were up to nine million native people in the Western Hemisphere. However, Native Americans had no knowledge of the existence of an Eastern Hemisphere, any more than the Europeans realized that the Americas existed. The two hemispheres were as different and independent as if they had actually existed on separate planets.

CHRISTOPHER COLUMBUS

6

AN EARLY VIEW OF THE HORRORS AWAITING SEAMEN AT THE EDGE OF A FLAT EARTH.

What Columbus did was to bring them *together*.

Today, we know that the world is a sphere with major land masses in the Eastern and Western hemispheres. Until the time of Columbus, however, the accepted view in Europe was that the world was flat like a plate, and that if you sailed far enough out on the ocean, you would fall off the edge. The "world" — the land mass upon which we lived — was surrounded by water, and that was that. Navigators like Columbus, who believed in the spherical world theory, were convinced they could reach the Far *East* by sailing *west*. Vikings, under the leadership of Lief Ericson (970-1020 AD) had settled briefly in Nova Scotia (they called it "Vinland") in or about 1000 AD, but they never realized that they had landed in another hemisphere. No, Columbus didn't "discover" America. However, he did demonstrate that the world was not flat, but spherical. Beyond this, for good or ill, he opened the way for the interaction between the two hemispheres.

Columbus was born in Genoa, a port city in Italy, where he grew up around ships and sailors. At that time, European trade with the Far East, which was principally carried on by Venetian traders who followed the route first discovered by Marco Polo, was flourishing, but Polo's overland route was extremely long and difficult.

Columbus was willing to undertake the potentially lethal experiment of sailing west to reach the East, and went in search of a government that would underwrite the cost of his adventure. He was turned down by the governments of the Italian city-states of Genoa and Venice, as well as Portugal. He next turned to King Ferdinand V (1452-1516) and Queen Isabella (1451-1501) of Castile in what is now Spain, who agreed to commit three ships — the *Nina*, *Pinta* and *Santa Maria* — and crews to the task. Columbus set sail on September 6, 1492 and, after a long voyage during which his sailors almost mutinied, the expedition landed at San Salvador in the West Indies on 12.

Columbus returned to Spain on March 15, 1493 and made subsequent voyages of colonization in 1493, 1500 and 1502. Columbus died in 1506, still believing that he had reached Asia. His discoveries were treated with enthusiasm by the Spanish authorities, who

A NORSE SEA CAPTAIN, CIRCA 1000 AD.

A HEARTY GROUP OF VIKINGS CELEBRATE THEIR LANDING IN "VINLAND."

energetically undertook an exploration and colonization effort that would ultimately lead to a survey of most of the Western Hemisphere's eastern coast within a generation, and the realization that Columbus had in fact discovered a "New World."

Despite the fact that his intentions were far from evil, Columbus was condemned in the late twentieth century by a vocal minority within the United States educational community who imagined him as a symbol of the European "invasion" of North America. Indeed, the true scope of Columbus' "discovery" or "invasion" could not be comprehended in his lifetime or for many years thereafter.

The reason for his being blamed in this way is probably that for many years, he was idealized and idolized in an equally unrealistic fashion, and that he became a symbol for an event. When the event was seen as a triumph, Columbus was a hero. In 1893, the 400th anniversary of his first voyage was the centerpiece of the Chicago World's Fair. When the event was perceived as having had a negative impact on the native people of North America, Columbus became a villain. In reality, he probably could not have comprehended himself in either role.

The controversial Columbus was the scion of a seafaring family. His education was undertaken with some care, but before reaching what in our times would be called graduation, he left off his studies and went to sea. He had a passion for the sailor's art and for adventure. There is in his life an obscure period of about 20 years, in which he traversed the Mediterranean, issuing at intervals through the Straits of Gibraltar. He visited the western ports of Europe and went to Iceland about 1470. It was here that he heard the Norse tales of new lands in the West, and he returned to Portugal and Spain, dreaming, we may presume, of a possibility of sailing westward to the East Indies.

For about 10 years he went from court to court begging for the support of their sovereigns for his transatlantic voyage. At last Columbus found an appreciative listener in the great Queen Isabella, who became a constant and faithful friend to the navigator, and never abandoned him to her dying day.

Having been fitted out under Isabella's command, the three ships of Columbus set sail into the literal unknown. Fear and apprehension almost led to mutiny, but in the morning light of October 12, 1492, a sailor on the *Pinta* sighted land. It was calendared, perhaps with truth, that Columbus had on the night before, at about 10 o'clock, seen a light at what was afterward supposed to be Cat Island. But the discovery of the following morn-

AN EARLY SIXTEENTH CENTURY VIEW OF NATIVE AMERICANS AND OF THE SANTA MARIA.

A FANCIFUL VIEW OF COLUMBUS LANDING IN SAN SALVADOR ON OCTOBER 12, 1492.

ing was clear and incontrovertible. The signal gun was fired and the ships lay to.

A landing party went ashore and was met by a group of Native Americans who came down to the shore to see their strange visitors. The two races stood face to face.

The people were identified by these Europeans as "Indians" because they inhabited what Columbus hoped and assumed were the East Indies. Though it was resolved within a generation that these were not the East Indies, the name "Indian" would continue to be used to identify the people of the New World, although in the late twentieth century, the more properly descriptive term "Native American" was adopted as an alternate name for the indigenous people of the Americas.

Within weeks of his San Salvador landing, Columbus made other discoveries. He visited the islands of Conception, Cuba and Hispaniola, and a fort was erected on the bay of Caracola on the latter island. Timbers salvaged when the Santa Maria was wrecked were used in the building of this first structure by Europeans in the New World.

Exploration continued for about three months, and during the first week of January, 1493, Columbus set sail for Spain, taking with him the indubitable proof of what he had found. He arrived in the month of March and was greeted with enthusiasm. Columbus was a hero,

COLUMBUS LANDED IN WHAT IS NOW HAITI IN 1493 DURING HIS SECOND VOYAGE.

A bearded Columbus reports his discoveries to Isabella and Ferdinand.

but his discovery in the West had not corresponded to his expectations. The Indies which he had found were not the Indies of Marco Polo.

On his second voyage, the discoverer had a respectable fleet and more mariners than he could take with him. He reached the Windward Group, and explored the coasts of Jamaica and Puerto Rico. A colony was established in Haiti, and Diego Columbus was appointed governor. This time, it was not until the summer of 1496 that Columbus returned to Spain.

This time, he discovered that his own subordinates had made false reports, and his fortunes and reputation had already begun to decline. He became the victim of jealousies and suspicions from which he never recovered. Persecution would follow him during the remainder of his life.

On his third voyage he found the island of Trinidad, traversed the Gulf of Para, and reached the mainland of South America not far from the mouth of the Orinoco River, which today forms the border between Columbia (named for Columbus) and Venezuela.

On his return voyage he visited Haiti, where he found his colony in a desperate condition. He attempted to restore order, but was seized by Francisco de Bobadilla, the cruel new governor who had been sent out from Spain, and who arrested Columbus and carried him back to Spain.

The Spanish court freed Columbus and he was sent on a fourth voyage in search of the still-elusive riches described by Marco Polo. In this, the fourth voyage was a failure, but Columbus did explore a great distance along the south side of the Gulf of Mexico.

His failure to find the riches that he sought were a deep disappointment. When he returned once more to Spain, he learned that Isabella, his steadfast friend and sponsor, was dead. That was the end of his career. He died in poverty

A DOCUMENT SAID TO BE COLUMBUS' OWN LETTER DESCRIBING HIS DISCOVERY.

at Valladolid, leaving his hopes and his fame to posterity.

Ironically, the name ultimately bestowed on the new land by the Europeans was not that of Columbus, but of another Italian named Amerigo Vespucci, a native of Florence, Italy. He was one of those who followed quickly in the wake of the Columbian discoveries.

In 1499 he reached the coast of South America, though the results of his voyage were not significant. In 1501 he made another voyage, and returned to Europe to publish the first general account of the discoveries made in the Western World. It was Vespucci who established the fact that the new islands and mainland on the western shores of the Atlantic were not the East Indies, but were another continent. This continent was henceforth called America and not Columbia.

The crossing of the Atlantic and the revelation of new islands and continents in the West electrified the lethargic spirit of Europe. No other event in the history of humankind had opened so large a prospect for enterprise and adventure. Spain, in particular, under whose auspices "the New World" had been found, burned with a zeal that could hardly be quenched.

THE DEATH OF COLUMBUS, AND AT TOP, HIS PORTRAIT AS COMMISSIONED BY ISABELLA.

SPANISH EXPLORATION

As soon as the importance of the New World became known, the kings of Spain and Portugal began to contend for what the first had found and the second had neglected to find. Pope Alexander VI was called in to settle the dispute, and in 1493 did so by issuing a bull (decree) whereby an imaginary line was drawn north and south in the Atlantic 300 miles west of the Azores (*see map on page 37*). All the islands and countries west of that meridian were given to Spain. Though the area had yet to be mapped, almost all of the New World — except present-day Brazil — lay in the Spanish zone.

Within 10 years after the death of Columbus, all the greater islands of the West Indies had been found by the Spanish, explored and colonized. In 1510, a colony was established on the mainland at Darien in what is now Panama. Three years later, Vasco Nuñez de Balboa (1475-1517), the Spanish governor at Darien, had learned from the native people that another great water lay not far to the west. On September 25, 1513, after a 25-day expedition, he climbed over the slight central range of the narrow isthmus, and from a hilltop he beheld the limitless body of water that he called the Pacific.

Balboa and his companions went down to the water's edge. Carrying in his

THE KING SENDING SHIPS TO THE NEW WORLD.

VASCO NUÑEZ DE BALBOA REACHED THE PACIFIC ON SEPTEMBER 25, 1513.

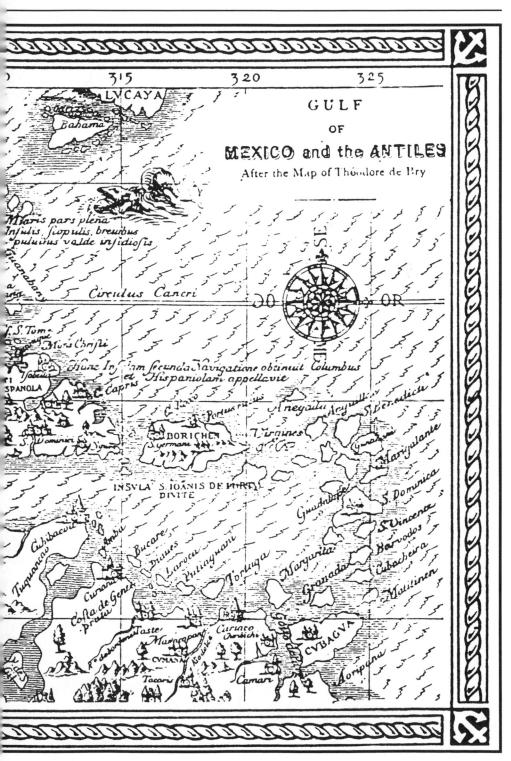

GULF

OF

MEXICO and the ANTILES

After the Map of Théodore de Bry

hand the banner of Spain, he waded in, in the pompous fashion of his age, and with drawn sword and flourish, he took possession of the great ocean in the name of King Ferdinand.

On his second voyage in 1493, Columbus had with him a lieutenant named Juan Ponce de León (1460-1521). He settled in Hispaniola, but became governor of Puerto Rico in 1509. In the meantime, a rumor had circulated in the Spanish colonies that somewhere in the islands of the Bahamas there was a fountain of eternal youth whose waters could prevent the aging process. The story appealed to the romantic sentiments of de León, and in the year 1512 he sailed from Puerto Rico in quest of the fabulous fountain. He went first to San Salvador and the neighboring islands, but then moved west, coming to an unknown coast on Easter Sunday.

De León supposed that he had found a new island. The shores were covered with a luxuriant forest. The horizon across the bright waters was banked with green leaves. Birds were heard singing there, and the fragrance of blossoms was wafted to the ships. The day on which the discovery was made was called in the calendar of the church Pascua Florida, or in Spanish, Pasqua de Flores. This notion caught the imagination of Ponce,

and he named the new shore Florida, the Land of Flowers. A landing was made a few days later, near the later city of St. Augustine. The Spanish banner and arms were planted, and the country claimed for Spain by the right of discovery.

Ponce de León explored the Land of Flowers, continuing his search for the fountain of youth. He went about bathing in many waters up and down the coast before giving up the quest and sailing back to Puerto Rico. The law of nature had prevailed over tradition. He was no younger than before.

Nevertheless, the discovery of Florida was of great importance, although it

A SIXTEENTH CENTURY SPANISH PORT.

would be some time before it was determined that the Island of Flowers was not an island, but the mainland of North America.

The king of Spain appointed Ponce de León as governor of Florida, and ordered him to colonize the country. The old adventurer was slow in doing this, and it was nine years after the discovery before he returned to his province. He found there the usual results of Spanish colonial ignorance and cruelty. The Native Americans had become irritated. When Ponce de León's colony debarked the natives attacked them and killed a great number, and the rest were obliged to run for their lives.

In order to save themselves, they took to their ship and sailed away. Ponce de León himself was struck with an arrow, mortally wounded and taken to Cuba to die. He had met his demise in the place in which he had searched for eternal life. The settlements established by the Spanish came and went, but one of the relatively later ones survives as the oldest continuously-inhabited European city in what is now the United States.

In 1565, a soldier of fortune named Pedro Melendez was commissioned by Philip II to colonize Florida. To this end, he was promised a large gift of land and a liberal salary. He gathered together a colony of 2,500 persons, and in July 1565 sailed from Spain. Melendez reached Florida on St. Augustine's Day and named the harbor and river in honor of that saint.

Meanwhile, on a site about 35 miles upstream, was the settlement of Fort Caroline, which had been established by a colony of Huguenots, French Protestants who came to Florida to escape religious persecution in France. Melendez attacked and destroyed the Huguenot settlement, and more than 700 of the colonists were massacred. Only a small number of servants and laborers would survive.

WARFARE BETWEEN THE SPANISH AND THE NATIVE AMERICANS OF FLORIDA.

SPANISH CONQUEST

The history of Europe has always been filled with the rise or fall of one or more political or economic powers. At the time that Columbus' discoveries became known in Europe, Spain and Portugal were on the threshold of coming to the fore as great trading nations, much like the Phoenicians had been 3,000 years before or as the British would become 400 years later.

Spain, via Columbus, had "discovered" the New World and moved quickly to exploit that untried, untested territory. Portugal, meanwhile, was more interested in trade with the Far East and in taking advantage of the route around the southern tip of Africa pioneered in 1498 by the Portuguese mariner Vasco da Gama (1469?-1524). Nevertheless, the Portuguese were swift to make claims in the Western Hemisphere. This led to the pope being asked to partition the New World between Spain and Portugal. Unfortunately for Portugal,

since the geography of the Western Hemisphere still remained largely unknown in 1494, the north-south demarcation line to which the two parties agreed gave Portugal only the easternmost part of the New World. This area later became Brazil, and today that nation remains the only country in the

SPANISH CONQUISTADOR HERNANDO CORTEZ.

22

AZTEC FOOT SOLDIERS WERE NO MATCH FOR THE SPANISH MOUNTED CAVALRY.

Western Hemisphere where Portuguese is the official language.

The Spanish expeditiously asserted their dominance over the rest of America south of the Caribbean as they sought to find El Dorado, the elusive — and probably mythical — "city of gold." In the course of their conquests, the Spanish conquistadors came into conflict with two of the most highly evolved civilizations in the New World — the Aztec Empire, centered at Teotihuaan in Mexico, and the Inca Empire, centered at Tiahuanaco, south of Lake Titicaca in what is now Bolivia. Both of these cultures had existed for 1,000 years, had built massive cities — Teotihuaan was the largest city in the world in 1500 — and had mastered mathematics, astrono-my and other sciences. They had not however, mastered the technology to match sixteenth century European war fare.

It was on the mainland of Mexico that the Spanish had their greatest impac on the history of North America. In 1517, Fernandez de Cordova sailed into the Bahia de (Bay of) Campeche and se foot on the Yucatan Peninsula. Exploring the northern coast, he was, like Ponce de León, attacked by the Native Americans and mortally wounded. In the following year, the coast of Mexico and Central America was extensively explored by Juan de Grijalva.

In 1519 Hernando Cortez (1485-1547) landed at Tabasco and began his brutal conquest of Mexico, the Empire

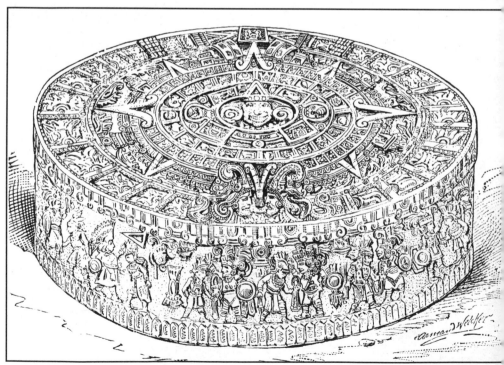

AZTEC ASTRONOMY WAS HIGHLY DEVELOPED, AND THEIR STONE CALENDARS WERE VERY PRECISE.

THE DEATH OF MONTEZUMA IN 1520 WHILE IN SPANISH CUSTODY.

of the Aztecs. Cortez established a beachhead on the coast and began to press his way westward. The native warriors by tens of thousands tried to stop the invaders, but could not. Riding horses and carrying firearms — both unknown to Native Americans — a relatively small number of conquistadors under Cortez met and defeated the Aztec forces. Mexican Emperor Montezuma (1480-1520) sent messengers to the Spaniards, counseling them not to advance. Cortez, however, was determined to do this, and he so notified Montezuma, saying that he wished to see him in person. On November 8, 1519, the Spanish entered the capital.

CORTEZ PROCLAIMS SPAIN'S EMPIRE IN MEXICO.

For a short time Cortez went about examining the city of Teotihuaan at will. He visited the altars and shrines where human sacrifices were made, inspected the defenses of the capital, and noted the methods of warfare employed by the Aztecs. He found vast treasures of gold and silver, limitless supplies of food, and arsenals filled with bows and javelins.

At length, though he was master and in the midst of splendor and abundance, Cortez began to feel alarmed about his situation. The Aztecs numbered millions and they had also become familiar with the invaders. They saw the Spanish cavalry dismount and no longer believed that the man and the horse were one. They learned that the Spaniards could be killed like other living things. Their courage rose, and there were signals of an insurrection. Cortez, sensing the danger, devised a scheme for seizing Montezuma and holding him as a hostage. When news came that the Aztecs at the coastal city of Vera Cruz had attacked the Spanish garrison, Montezuma was seized. He was compelled to acknowledge himself a dependent of the King of Spain, and he agreed to hand over large stocks of gold and silver as tribute.

For a while it seemed that Spanish dominion was firmly established in Mexico. Cortez, however, was soon imperiled by a movement in his rear. Valasquez, the Governor of Cuba, claiming to he superior in authority to Cortez, sent a force to Mexico to arrest his progress and to supersede him in command. The expedition was conducted by

Panphilo de Navarez (1478-1528), backed by a strike force of 1,200 heavily armed soldiers and Native American auxiliaries. Cortez, however, was on the alert. Leaving Pedro de Alvarado (1485-541) in command at Teotihuaan, Cortez took 200 commandos with him to meet the Navarez. On the night of May 26, 520, he burst into the camp of de Navarez at Vera Cruz, and compelled the whole force to surrender, inducing the conquered brigade, six times as strong as his own, to join him.

Meanwhile in Teotihuaan, affairs were in a desperate condition. The Aztecs had risen against Alvarado and cooped him up in a palace. When Cortez reached the city, he entered without serious opposition and rescued Alvarado's command, but the Aztecs could no longer be placated. Open warfare broke out. Thousands of the Aztecs were cut down in the streets and many of the Spaniards fell. For months there was incessant fighting in and around the city.

Cortez, to save his troops from destruction, compelled the captive Montezuma to go out into an exposed place and counsel his people to submit. In their rage and vexation, they let fly a shower of javelins, and Montezuma was fatally wounded. Cortez continued the siege, and the climax of a terrible conflict ended in the utter defeat of the Aztecs at Teotihuaan on August 14, 1521. The city was taken, the Empire of the Aztecs was extinguished and Mexico became a province of Spain.

Cortez's subsequent cruelty to the conquered Aztecs was matched only by that meted out by Francisco Pizarro 1471-1541) when he conquered the Incas of Peru in 1535. These two defeats of Native American empires by the conquistadors marked a milestone in world history. They were the first major conflicts between empires of the Old World and empires of the New World, and they were decisive.

They put the New World's vast mineral wealth, particularly that of Mexico, at Spain's disposal, making Spain the most powerful nation on Earth for the next 100 years. Perhaps most of all, these victories encouraged Spain's thirst to expand its holdings and led to it having the largest empire the Western Hemisphere would ever see. Today, 500 million people in the Western Hemisphere speak Spanish, at least half again more than speak English.

THE CRUEL FRANCISCO PIZARRO.

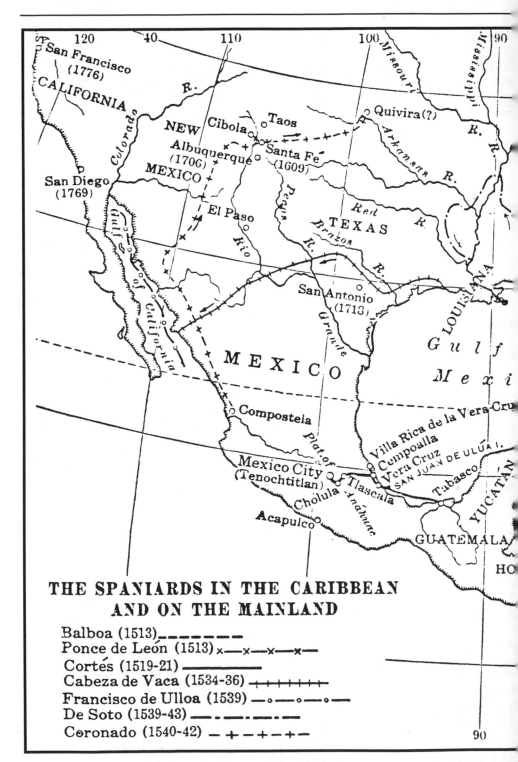

THE SPANIARDS IN THE CARIBBEAN
AND ON THE MAINLAND

Balboa (1513) _ _ _ _ _ _ _ _
Ponce de León (1513) x—x—x—x—
Cortés (1519-21) ——————
Cabeza de Vaca (1534-36) +++++++
Francisco de Ulloa (1539) —o—o—o—
De Soto (1539-43) —·—·—·—
Coronado (1540-42) —+—+—+—

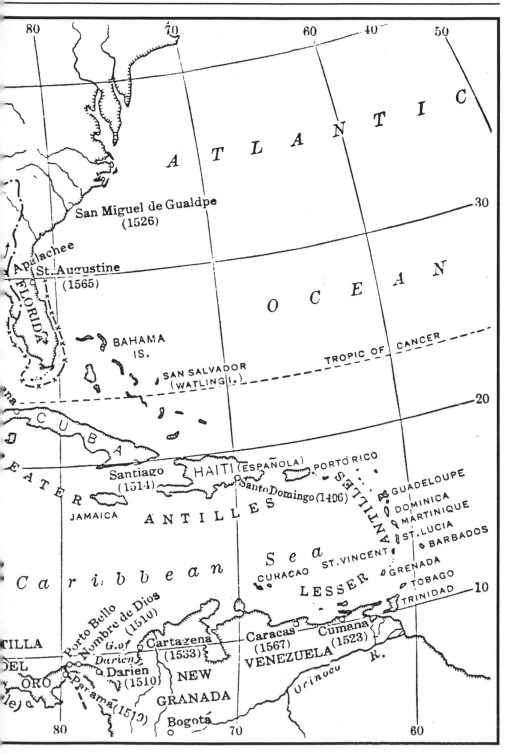

FIRST AROUND THE WORLD

B y the end of the fifteenth century, a growing minority of people had come to believe that the Earth was spherical like a globe rather than flat like a plate. Columbus had sought to prove this theory by sailing west to reach the East, and had in the process discovered a hemisphere previously unknown to Europeans. Three decades after Columbus completed his voyage of discovery, another adventurer, sailing under the Spanish flag, launched the expedition that eventually proved conclusively that the world was indeed a sphere.

Ferdinand Magellan (1480-1521) was born Fernao Magalhães in Sabrosa, Portugal, and served his king ably as a sailor and sea captain. By the dawn of the sixteenth century, it was clear that although Columbus had found a new continent, he had failed to find a western route to the East Indies. Magel-

lan tried, but failed, to interest the Portuguese government in financing a voyage to accomplish what Columbus had not, so he offered his idea and his services to Charles V of Spain, who accept-

MAGELLAN PUNISHING A MUTINEER.

ed. On September 20, 1519, Magellan set sail from Spain with five ships. Since no one had found a route through the center of the Western Hemisphere, he decided to sail around its southern edge. He traveled southwest and reached landfall near present-day Buenos Aires, Argentina by mid-October. He followed the coastline south and discovered a passage — a cold and rugged 360-mile trip around the tip of South America — on October 21. This passage, which connects the Atlantic and Pacific oceans, ever afterward was known as the Straits of Magellan, one of the roughest stretches of water on Earth.

When Magellan's ships emerged from the straits, he dubbed the relatively peaceful waters he encountered the "Pacific" Ocean. Sailing across the long, open stretches of the Pacific Ocean left the sailors short of food, and they landed in the Marianas Islands to take supplies aboard. The expedition arrived in the Philippines in April 1521, where Magellan himself was killed in a fight with the natives on April 27. The fleet, however, continued to sail westward, reaching the Moluccas and gathering there a cargo of spices. For the first time, Europeans sailing westward had come into known parts of the *East Indies*.

Weather and hardship took their toll, and eventually, all of Magellan's ships except one were damaged and could proceed no further. The remaining vessel took aboard the crews of the others and that lone ship sailed by way of the Cape of Good Hope and the western coast of Africa to Spain, where it arrived on September 17, 1522, having completed under the Spanish flag the first circumnavigation of the globe. The story of this history-making feat was told by Antonio Pigafetta, one of Magellan's sailors, in his book *The Voyage Around the World by Magellan*.

MAGELLAN'S LAST FIGHT, APRIL 27, 1521.

EUROPEANS BEGIN TO EXPLORE NORTH AMERICA

In 1539, Hernando de Soto (1496-1542), the Spanish governor of Cuba and Florida, undertook an expedition to explore the unknown lands to the north of the Gulf of Mexico. For three months they marched into the interior, swimming rivers, wading swamps and fighting Native Americans. October found them on Flint River, where they camped for the winter. In the following spring they set out in a northeasterly direction to find a great city ruled by an empress. The Spaniards reached into what is now South Carolina, and turned westward into the mountains of present-day North Carolina, Tennessee, northern Georgia and Alabama. They reached the Gulf Coast at Pensacola, where they met supply ships from Cuba.

De Soto then returned to the expedition, and on May 21, 1540, Native

DESOTO AND HIS EXPEDITION LANDING ON TAMPA BAY IN FLORIDA IN 1539.

American guides brought de Soto to a bluff overlooking the vast river we know today as the Mississippi, and which the Indians called "the Father of Waters."

Barges were built, and the Spaniards crossed into what is now Arkansas. They wintered on the Washita River, which they followed upriver to the Red River during the spring of 1541. De Soto's party then returned to the Mississippi and to the Gulf. Like Columbus, de Soto died without realizing the full importance of his discovery.

The door to European exploration and exploitation of the Western Hemisphere was opened by an Italian sailing under a Spanish flag, and this gave Spain an early lead in the New World, but they were by no means alone.

A great deal of enthusiasm prevailed at the other European courts when the news arrived that Columbus had returned from the western shores of the Atlantic. True, there was great confusion in the reports. The navigator himself supposed that he had found the East Indies which Marco Polo and other storytelling travelers had described as lying on the easternmost parts of Asia, but whatever it was, he had found land. Many islands had been circumnavigated. Others were so extensive as to seem to be continents.

Clearly this was but the beginning of an era of discovery. The imaginations were inflamed, incredulity was brushed aside, and a vast transatlantic rush began. All the maritime nations — notably France and England — immediately prepared to discover and to occupy the new lands in the West. The seafaring powers were quick to send their captains on the lines of discovery and adventure.

Among the many who were excited to ambition and activity by the great event of 1492 was another Italian navigator, Giovanni Gabotto, or Caboto, known to posterity as John Cabot (1450-1498). His birthplace was probably Venice, but his home was at Bristol, in the west of England. He was a seaman from his childhood. His voyages had reached to the easternmost parts of the Mediterranean. He had visited Mecca and had seen the incoming caravans from India laden with spices and gems. He believed, as Columbus did, that the Far East might be reached by sailing to

THE ROUTE OF DeSOTO'S EXPEDITION.

the west, and this notion he succeeded in impressing upon three English merchants of Bristol, who agreed to bear the expense of an expedition to be commanded by Cabot.

The consent of the Crown, however, was necessary. Henry VII, first king of England's House of Tudor, recently victorious over his enemies at the battle of Bosworth Field, was skeptical at first, but noted with great interest the discoveries that were being accomplished under the banners of Castile and León. In May 1496, he issued a charter to John Cabot, "Mariner, of Venice," granting him privilege and authority to make discoveries and explorations in the Atlantic and Indian oceans, to carry the English flag and to take possession of all islands and continents which he might discover. The expenses of the expedition were to be borne by the three merchants of Bristol, but one fifth of all the profits gained by the expedition should be given to the Crown.

The months of the following autumn and winter were spent in preparations for the voyage. Though a fleet of five vessels was prepared, only one ship, the *Matthew*, carrying a crew of 18 men under the immediate command of Cabot, sailed on the expedition. Among the crew were John Cabot's three sons, Lewis, Sebastian and Santius. On St. John's Day in June 1497, they reached Labrador, being the first Europeans in five centuries to set foot on the mainland continental mass of North America. Indeed, another 14 months elapsed before Columbus himself touched the mainland, and two years would pass before Vespucci traced the shore of South America.

Although it was summer, Cabot found the country which he had discovered to be ice-bound and wrapped in the

JOHN CABOT MAKES LANDFALL IN LABRADOR ON JUNE 24, 1497.

olitude of an apparently perpetual winter. The coast was forbidding, but a few Native Americans did come to see their ship. The shoreline was explored, however, for several hundred miles and Cabot imagined that he had found the kingdom of China, although neither the character of the country nor the appearance of the people supported this conclusion.

Before setting sail for England, Cabot, according to the terms of his commission, planted the flag of England and took possession in the name of the English king.

The *Matthew* returned to Bristol in August 1497. Cabot was received with rejoicing. An entry in the private accounts of Henry VII for the 10th of August is as follows: "For him that found the new isle, 10 pounds."

The cautious king issued a new commission, more liberal than the first, which was signed in February 1498. New ships were fitted and new crews enlisted for a second voyage.

Strange as it may seem, after the date of this second patent the very name of John Cabot disappears from the annals of the times. Where the remainder of his life was passed and the circumstances of his death are unknown, though he probably perished on the second voyage.

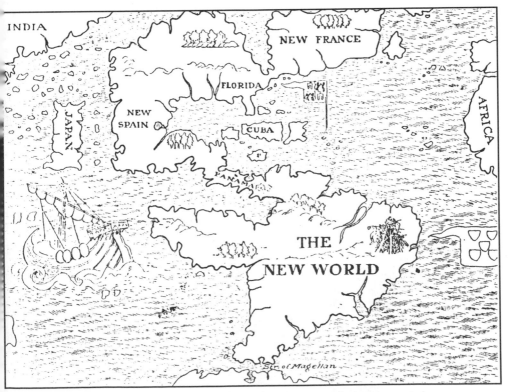

THE EUROPEAN VIEW OF THE SHAPE OF THE NEW WORLD IN 1540.

Sebastian Cabot (1474-1557), the second of John's sons, had inherited not only the plans and reputation of his father, but also his genius. Indeed, the younger Cabot appears through the shadows of four centuries as a man of greater capacity and enterprise. The younger Cabots had accompanied the elder on his famous first voyage, and Sebastian took up the cause with all the fervor of youth. It is probable that the same fleet, the equipment of which had been begun for the father, was entrusted to the son.

However this may be, Sebastian in the spring of 1498 found himself in com-

THE ENGLISH WARSHIP GREAT HARRY, LAUNCHED FOR HENRY VIII, HAD TWO TIERS OF GUNS.

nand of a flotilla of well-manned vessels and on his way to the new continent. At the close of the fifteenth century nothing was known about the general character of the great ocean currents which so largely modify the temperature of the seas and lands.

Navigators had no notion of the great difference in climate of the parts of Europe and America situated on the same parallels of latitude. The humidity and comparative warmth of England were naturally supposed to exist in the new lands at a corresponding distance north of the equator, and it remained for the Cabots to discover the much greater rigor of the climate on the western shores of the North Atlantic.

The voyage of Sebastian proceeded prosperously until he reached the seas west of Greenland. Here he was obliged by the icebergs to change his course. It was now July and the sun scarcely set at midnight. Seals were seen in abundance and the ships plowed through such shoals of cod as had never before been seen. The shore of Labrador was reached not far from the scene of John Cabot's earlier landing, and Sebastian turned southward, across the Gulf of St. Lawrence, or to the east of Newfoundland. His expedition explored New

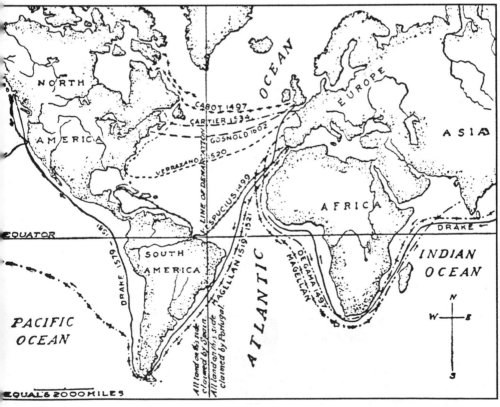

MAJOR EUROPEAN EXPEDITIONS TO AND AROUND THE AMERICAN CONTINENT (1497-1581).

Brunswick, Nova Scotia, and the coast of Maine.

The shoreline of New England was traced by European navigators for the first time since the days of the Norsemen. Cabot claimed lands as far south as Chesapeake Bay for the Crown of England, and it is probable that Cape Hatteras is the point from which Sebastian began his homeward voyage. It was in this manner that the right of England to the better parts of North America was first declared.

The "right" in question may be strongly criticized by posterity, as it rested wholly upon the fact of first view by a group of English sailors looking toward shore from their vessels in the summer of 1498. But this first view was called "discovery," and the kings of Europe had agreed among themselves that "discovery" would constitute a right which they would mutually respect and defend.

In this, there was not the slightest attention paid to the rights of *possession and occupancy* enjoyed for unknown generations by the native peoples of the "new" lands. All the claims of the Native Americans were brushed aside as not of consequence or validity. The flag of the Tudor dynasty had been carried in a ship along the coast from Labrador to Cape Hatteras, and English sailors had seen the New World before any of their European rivals. Therefore, England had a right to the possession of the continent thus "discovered."

As for Sebastian Cabot himself, hi future career was as strange as his voyages had been wonderful. The dark minded Henry VII, although quick to appreciate the value of Cabot's discoveries, was slow to reward the discoverer Cabot's accomplishments did not go unnoticed elsewhere. King Ferdinand the husband of the great Queen Isabella the patron of Columbus, enticed Sebastian Cabot away from England and made him Pilot Major of Spain. While holding this high office he undertook or oversaw many successful voyages to both North and South America.

KING HENRY VIII REIGNED FROM 1509 TO 1547.

At the beginning of the 1500s, the Spanish were certainly more interested in the character and possibilities of the New World than the English. During his tempestuous reign of nearly 40 years, Henry VIII was occupied with the domestic affairs of his kingdom, with threatening foreign intrigues which he resisted, and with the growth and greatness of England.

Against the turmoil, wars and cross purposes of Europe, Pope Alexander VI wielded tremendous respect and powers of mediation. His famous bull, intended to divide the New World (*see map on page 37*), actually gave Spain nearly all of the unexplored Americas except Brazil. In England, Henry VIII, always contending that he himself was the truest of Catholics, did not dispute the papal decision.

For this reason, the claims which had originated with the discoveries of the Cabots were allowed to lie dormant. The right of the English king to hold and possess the long continental line between Newfoundland and Carolina was not pressed by the first Tudor kings lest they should quarrel with the pope. It was not until after Henry's break with the Church in 1532, that the papal decision was fully rejected.

It was during the reign of Edward VI that there was a revival of English maritime adventure. When the break with Rome was once final, or seemed to be final, the decisions of the pope relative to the rights of the various European crowns were not likely to be much regarded by the ministers and advisers of young Edward. In 1548, his council voted 100 pounds sterling to induce the eminent Sebastian Cabot to quit Spain and become Grand Pilot of England. The old admiral yielded to the temptation, left Seville, and once again sailed under the English flag. The omens seemed auspicious for the speedy recovery of whatever England had lost to her rival by the apathy and indecision of half a century.

The beginning of the golden age of English sea power came with the reign

QUEEN ELIZABETH I RULED FROM 1558 TO 1603.

of Queen Elizabeth I (1533-1603), the daughter of Henry VIII and Anne Boleyn, who came to the throne in 1558. It was in 1588, during her time on the throne, that the English Fleet defeated the Spanish Armada, thus insuring that England would be the world's leading maritime power for the next three and a half centuries.

Elizabeth had in her the nature and disposition of a Catholic princess, but she came to power after her father's break with the Church and with the Catholic traditions that governed the great powers of Europe — France, Spain, Portugal and the Italian states. Thus her reign began against the backdrop of an estrangement with Europe and the accumulated ambitions of the House of Tudor.

England turned west across the Atlantic to the promising lands beyond. The spirit of discovery took form under the guiding hand of a bold and skillful sailor, Martin Frobisher of Doncaster. He received aid from Dudley, Earl of Warwick, who fitted out three small vessels and placed them under Frobisher's command. The goal of this expedition was a search of the rumored "Northwest Passage," a sea route around the northern edge of North America to the Pacific and Asia beyond. Three quarters of a century had already been invested in the notion of reaching the rich countries of the East by sailing around America to the

THE SHIPS USED BY MARTIN FROBISHER IN HIS 1576 EXPEDITION TO BAFFIN BAY.

north. It was a tantalizing theory, but in fact, the only sea route is the perpetually-frozen Arctic Ocean that was not navigable until the use of icebreakers and nuclear submarines in the latter twentieth century.

Frobisher departed in June 1576. One of his ships was lost on the voyage, and another ship's crew was terrified of the icebergs encountered, and returned to England. Nevertheless, the dauntless Frobisher proceeded to the north and west and discovered the group of islands which lie in the mouth of Hudson Strait. An inlet on Baffin Island still bears his name. Having visited several Inuit (Eskimo) villages, and having found a piece of gold ore, Frobisher confidently returned to England to happily report that he had discovered the mainland of Asia in what is actually the islands of northern Canada.

England was stirred to action by the excitement surrounding Frobisher's discovery of gold. Elizabeth I herself contributed a ship to the new fleet, which departed in May 1577. Frobisher's ships soon came among the icebergs of the far north, and for weeks they were in imminent danger of being crushed between the floating mountains. The summer was cold and unfavorable. The fleet did not succeed in reaching the same point to which Frobisher had sailed in his single vessel in the previous summer. The sailors were alarmed at the gloomy per-

ENGLAND'S 1588 DEFEAT OF THE SPANISH ARMADA CHANGED THE BALANCE OF WORLD POWER.

ils of sea and shore and availed themselves of the first opportunity to escape from these dangerous waters and return to England.

A third fleet of 15 vessels was fitted out, and Queen Elizabeth I again contributed personally to the expense of the voyage. In the early spring of 1578 the ships departed for the land of gold. It was the intention to plant there a colony of miners. Some were to remain, others to return with the fleet.

Twelve ships were expected to come back to England loaded with gold ore.But the third summer was as severe as the others. At the entrance to Hudson Strait, the floating icebergs were so thick that the ships could not be steered among them. The vessels were buffeted about in constant peril of destruction. At last,

they made landfall and began taking aboard the mineral resources that were available.

When the fleet returned to England, it was found that the ships' holds contained only dirt and virtually worthless mica — fools' gold! The Northwest Passage was forgotten. The colony which was to be planted was abandoned.

The English did not, however, abandon the idea of a transatlantic adventure. Rather, they turned to warmer latitudes, specifically those claimed by the Spanish. The hostility between the two powers amounted to almost constant war. Even when the Spanish and English crowns were nominally at peace and when Elizabeth and Spain's Philip II were exchanging cynical compliments, a state of conflict existed, which on the sea

IN 1579, SIR FRANCIS DRAKE WAS CROWNED AS THE "KING OF CALIFORNIA."

showed itself in many acts of violence and robbery.

It was at this time that the great English seaman Sir Francis Drake (1545-1596) came on the scene. Between 1567 and 1572, Drake operated as a pirate in the Caribbean, preying upon the merchant ships of Spain and thereby gained enormous wealth. In 1577, Queen Elizabeth I sponsored the great buccaneer on what was originally intended to be a search for the Pacific Ocean outlet of the Northwest Passage. The voyage was not successful in this regard, but it turned out to be an epic three-year expedition that would be the second after Magellan to circumnavigate the world.

In his 1577-1580 voyage aboard his ship *The Golden Hinde*, Drake sailed through the Straits of Magellan and followed the Pacific coast as far north as Oregon. He probably missed San Francisco Bay because of the fog, but he made landfall a few miles north, near Point Reyes, at a place still known as Drake's Bay. It was here that he built a fort, spent the winter and was crowned king by local Native Americans.

The first European to explore the western shores of what is now the United States, Drake claimed all that he surveyed for Queen Elizabeth under the name New Albion, but no permanent colony of Englishmen had been established. In 1579, Drake gave up on the search for the Northwest Passage and sailed south again in search of warmer waters. *The Golden Hinde* stayed in Mexico until the spring of 1580 before starting across the Pacific.

ELIZABETH I KNIGHTED DRAKE ABOARD HIS FLAGSHIP.

DREAMS OF AN ENGLISH OUTPOST IN AMERICA

Among the first English-men to devise a rational plan of colonizing North America was Sir Humphrey Gilbert. Having written a treatise on the possibility of finding a Northwest Passage to Asia, Gilbert began to consider the more realistic — yet still radical — idea of establishing an agricultural and commercial colony somewhere on the shores of the new continent. If the hope of finding gold had been elusive, he reasoned, certainly the hope of agriculture and commerce would not be.

Sir Humphrey brought his views to the attention of the queen and sought her aid. Elizabeth I reviewed his proposal favorably and issued to him a liberal patent authorizing him to take possession of any 600 square miles of territory in America, and to plant there a colony of which he himself should be proprietor and governor.

With this, Gilbert, assisted by his illustrious stepbrother, Walter Raleigh (1552-1618), prepared a fleet of five vessels, and in June 1583, they sailed for the West. Only two days after their departure, the best vessel in the fleet abandoned the rest and returned to England. Gilbert, however, continued his voyage, and early in August reached Newfoundland. Here he went ashore and took formal possession of the country in the name of Queen Elizabeth. Unfortunately some of the sailors discovered a mica deposit in the side of a hill, and it was decided that the mineral was actually silver ore. The crews became excited and at once went to digging the supposed silver and carrying it on board the ves-

SIR HUMPHREY GILBERT.

44

sels, while others commandeered the ships to attack Spanish and Portuguese vessels that were fishing for cod in the neighboring waters.

Sir Humphrey left Newfoundland and steered for the south with three ships. Off the coast of Massachusetts the largest of the remaining ships was wrecked and most of the crew lost. The disaster was so great that Gilbert gave up the expedition and set sail for England. The weather had become stormy and the two ships that remained were unfit. Sir Humphrey's ship, which was the weaker of the two, was a little frigate called *The Squirrel*. As the storm howled around them and the raging sea rose between them, *The Squirrel* was suddenly engulfed. Not a man of the courageous crew was saved. The other ship finally reached Falmouth in safety.

It would appear that these reverses and disasters rather quickened the ambitions than roused the fears of Sir Walter Raleigh. In the following spring the remarkable Raleigh obtained from the queen a new patent, fully as liberal as the one granted to Gilbert. Sir Walter was to be the Lord Proprietary of an extensive tract of land to he held in the name of the queen. A state was to be organized and populated by emigrants from England.

The character of the northern seas and coasts had now been sufficiently explored to turn the attention of explorers to a more hospitable region, specifically the sunny country extending from Cape Fear to the Delaware. Two ships were fitted out and the command given to Philip Amadas and Arthur Barlow. The expedition left England in April 1584, landed in the West Indies, and made its way up the coast of what is now the Carolinas. In July, they entered Ocra-

SIR WALTER RALEIGH.

coke Inlet. The coast was found to be long and low, the sea smooth and glassy. The woods were full of the beauty of native songbirds. The journal of Barlow is filled with exclamations of delight. The sailors seemed "as if they had been in the midst of some delicate garden."

The natives were found to be generous and hospitable. The ships sailed along the shores of Albemarle and Pamlico sounds before landing on Roanoke Island. After a stay of less than two months, they returned to England, praising the beauties of the new land. Elizabeth I, known as "the virgin queen" because she never married, gave this delightful new realm the name "Virginia."

Sir Walter Raleigh carried his own enterprise to Parliament. In December 1584 he secured the passage of a bill by which his former patent was confirmed and enlarged. Stories of Virginia captured public attention and the mind of the people was turned more to emigration. It was perceived by many that Sir Walter's proposed colony in the New World offered much in the way of opportunity, and colonization was taken up new with zeal and earnestness.

Raleigh fitted out a second expedition, appointing the soldier Sir Ralph Lane to be governor of the colony and the command of his fleet to Sir Richard Grenville. Sir Ralph was connected with the royal family and had been in the ser-vice of Mary and Elizabeth I for more than 20 years. Sir Richard was a naviga-tor from Cornwall, had been a soldier, a member of Parliament and had been knighted by Queen Elizabeth. He was also Raleigh's cousin, and he embarked eagerly on the project of colonization.

As for emigrants, they were made up to a considerable extent of the adventur-ous and gallant young nobility of the kingdom.

THE BAPTISM IN 1587 OF VIRGINIA DARE, THE FIRST ENGLISH CHILD BORN IN AMERICA.

The fleet, consisting of seven vessels, reached the Carolina shore in June 1585 when a storm arose and they were in imminent danger of destruction. This peril suggested to Grenville the naming of the nearby land as Cape Fear, a name which the outcropping on the coast has borne to the present day.

Escaping from the storm, the vessels came to the place where the colony was to be situated. One hundred and eight men were landed and organized by Governor Lane. For several days explorations were made in the neighborhood and then work began on the colony known as Roanoke.

Relations with the Native Americans got off to a bad start with the suspected theft of a silver cup. Sir Richard laid waste the fields of corn and burned a Native American town. He then set sail for England, taking with him a Spanish

SPANISH GALLEONS ATTACKED AND CAPTURED ENGLISH SUPPLY SHIPS EN ROUTE TO ROANOKE.

treasure ship which be had captured in the West Indies. Piracy and colonization went hand in hand.

The Native Americans were enraged at the cruelties of the Europeans. The spirit of gentleness which they had previously displayed toward the Europeans gave way to jealous suspicion and hatred. Lane and some of his companions were enticed with false stories to go on a gold hunting expedition into the interior. Their destruction was planned, and only avoided by a hasty retreat to Roanoke. The Native American chief was, in turn, lured into a trap and murdered. This crime, committed against the innocent Native Americans, opened a chasm of hostility that would haunt all the residents of North America for over 300 years.

Soon after, a shipload of supplies arrived from the prudent Raleigh, but the captain found no colony. The vessel, therefore, could do nothing but return. Two weeks later Sir Richard Grenville came in person to Roanoke with three well-laden supply ships and made a fruitless search for his colonists. All were gone. Not to lose possession of the colony altogether, the governor left 15 men on the island and set sail for home.

The general mood in England was discouraging. The ardor of the people cooled when it was known that the Roanoke experiment had ended in disaster. Nevertheless, truthful descriptions of the magnificent coast of Virginia and Carolina had now been published, and it was only a question of time before the spirit of enterprise and adventure would be revived. Sir Walter himself did much to promote and encourage emigration. In April 1587, a new fleet departed from England. The dangerous capes of Hatteras and Fear were avoided and the ship came safely to Roanoke. A search was made for the 15 men who had been left there a year before, but they too had been murdered by the now-hostile Indians. Nevertheless, Captain John White selected the northern extremity of Roanoke Island as the site for his "city," and on July 23, the foundations were laid.

But fortune was still adverse to the enterprise. The new settlers and the Native Americans renewed their hostilities and went to war. After some destruction and loss of life, peace was concluded, and Sir Walter conceived the plan of uniting the fortunes of the two races by common interest. He attempted to use Manteo, the Native American chief of Roanoke, as the link of union between the English and the natives. Manteo was recognized as one of the rulers of the land, and was made a peer of England with the title of Lord of Roanoke, a title which was meaningless from the point of view of the Indians.

As autumn came, the colonists were gloomy and apprehensive. They pretended to fear starvation and became half mutinous and almost compelled Governor White to return to England for additional supplies and new immigrants. The governor yielded to the pressure and sailed away. Had the colonists been content to employ the summer in useful labor, planting and gathering, they might have easily provided for themselves through the winter, but they imagined that their supplies must be constantly replenished from England.

One of the most notable events of that summer was the birth on August 18, 1587 of Virginia Dare, the first English child born in the New World. Spirits may have been buoyed by this milestone, for when White set sail for England, he left the 107 immigrants plus the native-born Virginia in full expectation of ultimate success.

It was not to be. Because of English preoccupation with the battle against the Spanish Armada in 1588, it was not until the spring of 1590 that Governor White finally returned to Roanoke. He found the island deserted and silent. No soul remained to tell the story of the lost colony of Roanoke. The only clue was the word "*Croatoan*," the name of a nearby Indian tribe, carved on a tree. The nature of their fate has never been ascertained.

Sir Walter Raleigh had spent a fortune of his own money in the attempt to found and foster a colony in America. Having failed, he gave up and assigned his proprietary rights to an association of London merchants.

It would be almost two decades before the effort at American colonization succeeded.

JOHN WHITE RETURNED TO ROANOKE IN 1590. THE PEOPLE HAD VANISHED, LEAVING ONLY THE MYSTERIOUS WORD "CROATOAN" CARVED ON A TREE.

EARLY EXPLORATION IN THE FAR WEST

Most discussion of the exploration and colonization in what is now the United States focuses on the Eastern Seaboard: the Spanish in Florida, the French in the St. Lawrence country and the English in between. However, there were expeditions to and within the Far West that involved important discoveries and led to the founding of settlements that have grown into major modern cities.

Even before Sir Francis Drake dropped the anchor of *The Golden Hinde* in Drake's Bay north of San Francisco Bay, Spanish expeditions were reaching north out of Mexico into what are now the states of New Mexico, Arizona and California.

By 1520, only 28 years after Columbus had first set foot in the Western Hemisphere, Hernando Cortez had defeated the Aztecs and the Spanish were the rulers of Mexico and a vast empire stretching into South America. The coastline had been, or was being, explored, but there was also a great deal of interest in the interior. The Aztec gold and silver mines were a reality. The Spanish found some and they wanted more.

While the English, French and later Dutch mariners were interested in finding the Northwest Passage to China and the Far East, the Spanish in Mexico were pursuing another, equally elusive dream. By the 1530s, stories were circulating in Mexico that told of a series of golden cities in what is now the Ameri-

WOMEN OF THE HOPI TRIBE.

an Southwest, called the Seven Cities of Cibola. These cities were wealthy beyond belief, so much so that the walls of all the buildings were sheathed in sheets of pure gold.

In 1536 Cabeza de Vaca and three companions arrived in Mexico City, sole survivors of the shipwrecked Navarez Expedition, after eight years of wandering through what is now the American Southwest. They told a wild tale of a land with "large cities, with streets lined with goldsmith shops, houses of many stories and doorways studded with emeralds and turquoise!"

In 1539 Antonio de Mendoza, the Viceroy of New Spain (Mexico), sent the friar Fray Marcos de Niza with some guides and Estévan, a black man who had been with Vaca, to verify the story. Fray Marcos returned within the year with a glowing report of the "Seven Cities of Cíbola." Estévan, however, had been killed by the Native Americans.

The Viceroy then began planning an official expedition and chose his friend Francisco Vásquez de Coronado (1510-1554), to lead it. He cautioned Coronado that the expedition was to be a missionary undertaking, not one of conquest.

They left on February 23, 1540 with 336 Spanish soldiers, four priests, including Fray Marcos, several hundred Mexican Indian allies and 1,500 stock animals. Supplies were sent north by ship. After reaching Culiacán, Coronado and 100 soldiers marched ahead of the main army and on July 7, 1540 reached Háwikuh, the first of the fabled Cities of Cíbola.

Instead of a golden city, they found a rock-masonry pueblo crowded with Native Americans who were ready to fight. The Spaniards attacked and forced the Indians to abandon the village. The pueblo, well stocked with food, became Coronado's headquarters until November 1540.

THE ANCIENT MESA-TOP HOPI CITY OF TEWA IN NORTHEAST ARIZONA.

While at Háwikuh, Coronado sent his captains out to explore. Don Pedro de Tovar discovered the Hopi Indian villages in northeastern Arizona, and Garcia López de Cardenas "discovered" the Grand Canyon of the Colorado River and explored the strange and geologically fantastic terrain of the Southwest.

Coronado found the Seven Cities, but they turned out not to be solid gold. In fact, they were the great adobe pueblos of the Rio Grande Valley that still exist in the area around present-day Albuquerque and Santa Fe, and which are still inhabited by descendants of the people who lived there when Coronado arrived.

Indeed, the Seven Cities of Cibola were probably the Rio Grande and northern Arizona pueblos with the brilliant late afternoon sun illuminating them *as though they were made of gold*!

The northernmost of these cities, the Taos Pueblo, is one of the largest, and to this day, one of the best preserved. Another, the "Sky City" at Acoma near Albuquerque, was over 900 years old in Coronado's time and is the oldest continuously-inhabited city in what is now the United States.

A third Coronado expedition captain, Hernando de Alvarado, and 20 men traveled east, through the upper Rio Grande Valley and into the country of the the upper Pecos River. Here they met a plains Indian they called "the Turk." He astounded them with tales of the great trading center in the middle of what is now New Mexico, which was later known by the Spanish name "Gran Quivira."

The following spring, on April 23, 1541, they set out to find Quivira, guided by the Turk. After 40 days, Coronado

HOMES AND KIVAS (CEREMONIAL ROOMS) AT THE WALPI PUEBLO IN ARIZONA.

CORONADO VISITS A TENTH CENTURY CLIFF DWELLING IN NEW MEXICO.

sent most of his men back to Tiquex and continued on with only 30 men. Coronado failed to reach Gran Quivira. Uninhabited since the late seventeenth century, Gran Quivira was the key point of contact between the Native Americans of the Southwest and the Plains tribes at the time Coronado visited the region.

Although Coronado never found the *golden* Seven Cities of Cíbola, he and his men had found the Grand Canyon, as well as having met many Hopi, Zuni, and other peoples along the Rio Grande. Coronado reached as far north as Nebraska and had contact with the Arapahoe, Caddo, Cheyenne, Comanche, Kiowa and perhaps the Sioux (Dakota) people.

Coronado's men were the first Europeans to see buffalo, which he called "hump-backed cattle."

Coronado had met with Native Americans who lived in large permanent cities, and he met nomadic Native Americans who lived in cone-shaped buffalo-hide houses called tepees, but he found no cities of gold and he was disappointed.

Coronado returned to Mexico City at the end of 1542, empty-handed and with only half of the troops with whom he had set out. Like the French and English on the Eastern Seaboard, the Spanish did not give up. They came back, established trading posts and missions and eventually found gold, although it was in the mines worked by Native Americans and it was present in smaller quantities than hoped. In 1582, Spanish mis-

sionaries exploring the Verde Valley in Arizona recorded that Native Americans were using the copper mines near what is now Jerome. Their description matches the actual mines that were found in 1883 by miners of the United Verde Company. The first Spanish farms were established in the Gila River Valley in Arizona by Jesuit missionary Father Eusebio Francisco Kino in 1699.

Santa Fe, in the upper Rio Grande Valley and now the state capital of New Mexico, was established during the winter of 1609-1610 by Don Pedro de Peralta. As such it followed the English settlement at Jamestown by only two years and is older than any continuously-inhabited cities founded by the English anywhere on the Eastern Seaboard.

THE MOQUI PUEBLO.

The Pacific was first seen from the Americas by European eyes in about 1510, although Vasco Nuñez de Balboa, the Spanish governor of Darien (Panama), gets the credit for having "discovered" it in 1513. It was in this year that he took possession of the great ocean in the name of King Ferdinand, and it was soon after that attempts were made to explore the coastline.

The first European expedition to set foot on the Pacific shore of what is now the continental United States was probably that of Juan (Juao) Rodriguez Cabrillo (?-1543). A Portuguese captain sailing under the Spanish flag, Cabrillo made landfall in San Diego Bay in September 1542 and explored much of the coast of Southern California. Sir Francis Drake arrived in 1577-1580 during a voyage aboard *The Golden Hinde*.

Sir Francis Drake had sailed through the Straits of Magellan and followed the Pacific coast as far north as Oregon. He probably missed San Francisco Bay because of the fog, but he made landfall a few miles north, near Point Reyes, at a place still known as Drake's Bay. It was here that he built a fort, spent the winter and was crowned king by local Native Americans (*see page 42*).

He claimed California for Queen Elizabeth I under the name New Albion, but the English never enforced this claim to the West Coast.

In 1602, the Spain's explorer Sebastian Vizcaino (1550-1615) made a systematic survey of the California coast as far north as Cape Mendocino. He noted the splendid harbor at what is now Monterey, but like Cabrillo and Drake, he missed the Golden Gate, the entrance to San Francisco Bay. It would not be until 1769, during their first major push to colonize California, that Spain would discover this unparalleled natural harbor.

CABRILLO UNLOADING HORSES IN CALIFORNIA. HORSES WOULD REVOLUTIONIZE NATIVE CULTURE.

THE FRENCH TURN TO THE NEW WORLD

Among the European powers to send expeditions to North America and the Caribbean in the century after Columbus, the Spanish and English were the first and the most persistent, but they were not alone. Certainly the government of France at the close of the fifteenth century could afford to patronize and encourage such adventures.

In fact, as early as 1504 the fishermen of Normandy and Brittany began to sail as far west as the banks of Newfoundland. A map of the Gulf of St. Lawrence was drawn by a Frenchman in 1506, and two years later, a French ship kidnapped several Native Americans and carried them to France for the astonishment of the court of Louis XII.

In 1518 Francis I became the first King of France to formally consider the project of colonizing the New World. However, the riches of Asia still beckoned, and Francis joined the ranks of European monarchs who dreamed longingly and greedily of a Northwest Passage around the northern edge of North America. In 1523 Francis I's first search for the passage began. A voyage of discovery and exploration was planned with Giovanni Verrazano (1485-1528), a native of Florence, appointed to head the expedition.

It was near the end of the year that Verrazano left Dieppe, on the frigate *Dolphin*, to begin his voyage. He reached the Madeira Islands, where he paused until January of the following year. The weather was unfavorable, the sailing difficult, and it required nine weeks of hard struggle against wind and wave to bring him to the North American coast near present-day Wilmington, Delaware.

Coasting northward, Verrazano discovered New York and Narragansett bays. At intervals he made landfall and opened a dialogue with the Native Americans, who he reported to be gentle and confiding. A Frenchman who was washed ashore by the surf was treated by them with great kindness and was permitted to return to the ship.

On the coast of Rhode Island, perhaps in the vicinity of Newport, Verrazano anchored for 15 days and there continued his trade with the Indians. Before leaving, however, the French sailors repaid the confidence of the

THE LEGENDARY SEAMAN JACQUES CARTIER.

Native Americans by kidnapping a child and attempting to kidnap one of the young women of the tribe.

Verrazano then continued along the coast of New England for a great distance. The Native Americans in this part of the country were wary and suspicious. They would buy neither ornaments nor gadgets, but were eager to purchase iron, knives and other weapons. Verrazano reached Newfoundland in the latter part of May, taking possession in the name of the King of France.

On his return to Dieppe, in July of 1524, he wrote a rather rambling account of his discoveries for Francis I. His work, however, was formally recognized by the sovereign, who gave the name New France to that part of the coastline which had been traced by the adventurous crew of the *Dolphin*. Meanwhile, the political situation in Europe at the close of the first quarter of the sixteenth century had become unfavorable for carrying out colonization abroad. The Reformation had broken out in Germany.

Three great monarchs, Francis I of France, Henry VIII in England and Charles V of Spain, had amassed power that had not been attained since the days of Charlemagne in the ninth century. Mutual jealousy supervened among these powerful men. Each watched the others with concealed animosity and dread. On the whole, Francis I and his government suffered the most in the contest of cross-purposes.

Against this backdrop, 10 years elapsed after the discoveries and explorations of Verrazano before another expedition could be sent out from France.

In 1534, Philippe de Chabot, admiral of the Kingdom of France, selected Jacques Cartier (1491-1557), a sea captain from St. Malo, in Brittany, to make France's second major official voyage to America. Two ships were equipped, and after no more than 20 days of sailing under cloudless skies, they dropped anchor on the 10th of May off the coast of Newfoundland.

Like his predecessors, Cartier had hoped and even expected to discover, somewhere in these waters, a passage westward to Asia. While this would never be, he greatly expanded the horizons of what Europeans knew about the geography of North America. By the middle of July, Cartier had circled Newfoundland, crossed the Gulf of St. Lawrence, found the Bay of Chaleurs and had followed the coast as far as Gaspe Bay. It was here that he proclaimed the King of France to be monarch of the land he had surveyed.

AN EARLY VIEW OF NOVA SCOTIA, NEWFOUNDLAND AND THE GULF OF ST. LAWRENCE.

Cartier sailed up the St. Lawrence River, but decided it to be impracticable to pass the winter in the New World. Cartier turned his prow toward France, and in 30 days he had reached St. Malo in safety.

The news of his voyage and its results produced a great deal of excitement. As had been the case in England, the young nobility of France became ambitious to seek their fortune in the New World.

Another flotilla of three vessels was fitted out and the sails were spread by zealous hands on May 19, 1535. Because of heavy seas the coast of Newfoundland was not reached until August. It was the feast day of St. Lawrence, so the name of the martyr was accordingly given to the gulf and river that still bear the name

JACQUES CARTIER SURVEYS THE ST. LAWRENCE VALLEY FROM THE TOP OF MONT REAL.

The ships sailed upriver to the island of Orleans, where the ships were moored.

Two Native Americans of the Huron tribe who had accompanied Cartier to France now told of an important town farther upriver on an island called Hochelaga. Indeed, it was a beautiful village at the foot of a high hill in the middle of the island. Climbing to the top of the hill and viewing the scene, Cartier claimed the island for the King of France, and named the town Mont Real (Royal Mountain). Today, the city of Montreal is the largest city in Canada and the second largest French-speaking city in the world.

This time, the French decided to winter in the New World, but disease and bitter cold took their toll. During the winter, 25 of the French died of scurvy, a malady hitherto unknown in Europe. Other hardships came with the season. Snows and excessive cold prevailed for months together. Unaccustomed to the rigors of such terrible weather, the French sailors and would-be colonists decided to return to France when spring came.

THE FRENCH CAME IN SEARCH OF GOLD, BUT UNLIKE THE SPANISH, THEY WERE DISAPPOINTED. INSTEAD, THEY DISCOVERED THAT THE RICH PELT OF THE NORTH AMERICAN BEAVER WAS WORTH ITS WEIGHT IN GOLD TO SATISFY THE EUROPEAN DEMAND FOR FURS.

However, before the ships left their anchorage, the chief of the Huron people, who had treated Cartier and his men with great generosity, was enticed aboard and carried off to France, where he would die.

When the fleet reached St. Malo, the accounts which Cartier was able to give of the new country and his experiences caused as much discouragement as his previous voyage had caused excitement. Neither silver nor gold had been found on the banks of the St. Lawrence. The rhetorical question that seemed to be asked was, "What was a New World good for that had not silver and gold?"

In 1541, Francois de la Roque, Lord of Roberval in Picardy, revived the project of planting a French colony beyond the Atlantic. He was given the titles of Viceroy and Lieutenant General of New France, and received from the court of France a commission to make an expedition to the country of the St. Lawrence. However, despite his elaborate titles, Roberval was wise enough to avail himself of the experience and abilities of his predecessor.

Cartier was retained in the service and induced to conduct the new expedition with the titles of Chief Pilot and Captain General.

JACQUES CARTIER PERSUADING THE CHIEF OF THE HURONS TO ACCOMPANY HIM TO FRANCE.

However, Roberval had difficulty in securing a sufficient number of emigrants. He appealed to the court for aid. The government responded by opening the prisons of the kingdom and giving freedom to whoever would join the expedition. There was a rush of robbers, swindlers and murderers, and the expedition was immediately fully staffed. Only counterfeiters and traitors were denied the privilege of gaining their liberty in the New World.

Five ships under Cartier's command left France — without Roberval, who said he'd come later — in May 1541. They reached the St. Lawrence in good condition and proceeded to the present site of the city of Quebec, where a fort was erected and dubbed Charlesbourg. Here the colonists spent another difficult winter.

Cartier, offended at his subordinate position, was not committed to the success of Roberval's colony, so when the Viceroy and Lieutenant General of New France arrived on a supply ship in June 1542, Cartier secretly got together his own part of the flotilla and returned to Europe. Roberval found himself alone in New France with three shiploads of criminals.

Instead of working to establish his colony, the viceroy spent his time trying to discover the Northwest Passage. The winter was one of gloom, despondency and suffering, so the following spring-was welcomed by the colonists as an opportunity to return to France. Thus the enterprise which had been undertaken with so much pomp came to naught. In 1549 Francois de la Roque again gathered a large group of emigrants and renewed the project. The expedition departed under favorable skies, but the ships were never seen again.

The effect of these failures meant that a half century would elapse before the effort to colonize America was renewed by the French government. Meanwhile, private enterprise and religious persecution worked together to accomplish in Florida and the Carolinas what the government of France had failed to accomplish on the St. Lawrence.

The first attempts by the French to establish full-fledged colonies in North America occurred at roughly the same

*ROBERVAL VANISHED IN THE ARCTIC IN **1549**.*

time that the English were starting to look into doing the same in Virginia.

By the middle of the sixteenth century, Protestantism had appeared in France, and followers of this faith had begun to suffer at the hands of the king and the Church. Gaspard de Coligny (1519-1572), leader of the French Huguenots, and then serving as Admiral of France, conceived of establishing a refuge for his persecuted fellow countrymen in America.

The king was willing for the Huguenots to leave the country, so in 1562, Coligny obtained from Charles IX a charter for the establishment of a French Protestant colony in the New World. Jean Ribault of Dieppe, a brave and experienced captain, was selected to lead the Huguenots to the land of promise, and a group of the exiles was soon collected. Their ships reached the coast of Florida in safety and sailed up the St. Johns River, which they called the River of May.

The fleet then sailed north to the entrance of Port Royal and the colonists went ashore on an island, and a stone engraved with the arms of their native land was set up to mark the place. A fort was built and the land was dedicated as Carolina in honor of Charles IX. Here Ribault left a garrison of 26 men and returned to France for additional emigrants and supplies.

However, civil war was now raging in the kingdom, and it was impossible to procure the needed supplies or other

DOMINIC DE GOURGES AVENGED THE 1565 MURDER OF FRENCH HUGUENOTS BY THE SPANISH.

emigrants. Meanwhile, the men left in America became anxious with the long wait, killed their leader, constructed a crude ship and put to sea. They were driven at the mercy of the winds and waves, but were at last picked up, half starved, by an English ship and were carried back to France.

Admiral Coligny, however, resolved to build a second colony and appointed Rene de Laudonniere to head the venture. Again the colonization effort was a failure. A settlement known as Fort Caroline was built on the St. Johns River, but the immigrants which remained were restless. Under the pretense of an escape from famine, a group contrived to get possession of two of the ships and sailed away. Instead of returning to France, however, they became pirates and had an extensive crime spree before they were caught, brought back and hanged. The rest of the settlers were on the verge of breaking up the colony when Ribault, who had commanded the first expedition, arrived from France with a cargo of supplies.

In 1565, Pedro Melendez, the Spanish governor of Florida, discovered the whereabouts of the French Huguenot settlement in Florida. Regarding them as intruders in the territory of Spain, Melendez attacked and destroyed the settlement, and more than 700 of the colonists were massacred.

The news of this atrocity created great sorrow and indignation among the Huguenots in France. Dominic de Gourges (Dominico Gorges), a soldier of fortune from Gascony, prepared to avenge the death of his countrymen. He planned an expedition against the Spanish settlements in Florida and soon came down upon them with a brutal vengeance. With three ships and only 50 seamen he arrived in midwinter on the coast of Florida. With this handful he surprised the three forts on the St. Johns River and made prisoners of the garrisons. Unable to hold his position, he condemned and hanged his leading captives from the branches of trees, putting up the description "Not Spaniards, but murderers."

It was not until 1598 that the attention of the French government was once more directed to the claims which the early navigators had established to ports on the American coast. The Marquis de la Roche, a nobleman of influence and distinction, took up the cause and obtained a commission authorizing him to found an empire in the New World. Unfortunately the colony was again to be made up by opening the prisons and granting immunity to those inmates who would emigrate.

This time the destination was Nova Scotia, specifically Sable Island, described as a place of desolation and gloom. Here the marquis left 40 men to found the colony while he returned to France for a cargo of supplies. Unfortunately for those left behind, the marquis died soon after his arrival at home. For several dreary years, the new French Empire, composed of 40 convicts, languished on Sable Island. At last they were mercifully picked up by passing ships and carried back to France. It was reckoned by the authorities that the punishment of the poor wretches had been sufficient and they were never remanded to prison.

At last, however, the time came when a permanent French colony would be established in America. In 1603, the government of France granted the sovereignty of the country from the latitude of Philadelphia to one degree north of Montreal to the French count Pierre du Guast, commonly known as De Monts. He received from the king a patent giving him a monopoly of the fur trade in the area, and conceding religious freedom for Huguenot immigrants.

In March of the following year De Monts sailed from France with two shiploads of colonists and reached the Bay of Fundy. The summer was spent trading with the Native Americans and exploring the northwest coast of Nova Scotia, where they found an excellent harbor at the mouth of the St. Croix River. It was here that they built a rude fort. Established in November 1605 and called Port Royal, this would be the foundation of the first permanent French settlement in North America.

It was at this time that an explorer and soldier of fortune named Samuel de Champlain (1567-1635) appeared on the scene. In 1603 he had been commissioned by a group of merchants in the French city of Rouen to explore the St. Lawrence region and establish a trading post. By this time, it had been discovered that the abundant furs of the area were a surer source of riches than the mines of gold and silver that had proven impossible to find.

Champlain reached the St. Lawrence, and the site where Quebec now stands was chosen as the place for a fort. In the autumn the leader returned to France and published a favorable

SAMUEL DE CHAMPLAIN

account of his enterprise. It was not for five years, however, that Champlain finally returned to America. On July 3, 1608, the foundations of Quebec were laid.

In 1609 Champlain and two other French adventurers joined with the Huron people, then at war with the Iroquois of New York. It was during this war that Champlain traveled up the Sorel River to discover the narrow lake which now forms the border between the states of Vermont and New York, and which has borne his name ever since.

By 1624, with the foundation of the fortress of St. Louis, the permanence of the French settlements — including the nuclei of both Montreal and Quebec — in the valley of the St. Lawrence was at last assured.

French explorers and traders sailed up the St. Lawrence and navigated the Great Lakes, and Etienne Brule (1592-1632) reached the Lake Superior area by

1623. Louis Joliet (1645-1700) and Father Jacques Marquette (1637-1675) traveled as far as present-day northeast Iowa while exploring the Wisconsin and Mississippi rivers in 1673. Others soon followed — exploring, building forts, and developing Native American trade.

During the century and a half that France was active in North America, her explorers, fur traders, missionaries and soldiers spread through the interior of the continent via the St. Lawrence, Great Lakes and Mississippi waterways. Although the French made a general claim of sovereignty over lands of the interior, they did nothing to disturb the Indians' actual possession of them, aside from establishing small forts and posts. The most important of these settlements were Detroit, Kaskaskia, Cahokia, and Vincennes, whose populations included military officers and wealthy traders, and a lower class of smaller traders, farmers, and artisans. Indeed, the quest for beaver was very important, and the fur trade with the Indians dominated the economy and much of the daily activity.

They lived among the Native Americans and, as the generations passed, French people intermarried with most of the tribes of the upper plains and Great Lakes area.

The French arrived in the New World eager to take to the woods and enter the lucrative fur trade. The roving French *coureur de bois* and *voyageurs* soon became a vital part of the North American frontier.

A SIXTEENTH CENTURY DINNER PARTY AT THE FRENCH FORT AT PORT ROYAL.

THE DUTCH IN NORTH AMERICA

J ust as the papal bull of 1493 divided the New World vertically between Spain and Portugal, the essential pattern of exploration divided eastern North America laterally between Spain, England and France. While Spain was the major player in Central and South America, it played a minor role in eastern North America, except in Florida. From Florida to the St. Lawrence the English would predominate, and in the St. Lawrence country it was the French.

The Dutch, a major seafaring people, would also play an important — though small and short-lived — role in the development of European settlement in eastern North America. Most important, they would found the settlement that evolved into the largest city in North America.

The story of Dutch settlement in America begins with the illustrious Henry Hudson (1565-1611), an English-born Dutch sea captain. The year 1607 found him employed by a group of London merchants, who'd commissioned him to search for, not that most elusive of New World dreams, the Northwest Passage, but a *Northeast* Passage. On his 1607 voyage, made with a single ship, Hudson had already endeavored to circumnavigate Europe to the northeast. He succeeded in reaching the island of Spitzbergen north of Norway, but was obliged by the rigor of the ice-choked seas to return to England.

The following year, he renewed the voyage, but was unable to find the "Northeast Passage." With this, the London group declined further support, so the undaunted Hudson turned to the Netherlands. At this time, the powerful commercial corporation known as the Netherlands East India Company, based in Amsterdam, was actively working toward the goal of exploiting the riches of the East Indies, so Hudson was just the sort of man they were looking for.

The officers of the Netherlands East India Company liked this sturdy captain whom they called "Hendrick" Hudson (using the Dutch equivalent of Henry). They assigned him a small ship called *Half Moon*, and directed him to continue his search for an all-water route to the Indies. In April 1609 he sailed north of Norway, reached 72 degrees north latitude and turned eastward, but was turned back by the icebergs. Perceiving that it

HENRY "HENDRICK" HUDSON.

Americans bringing gifts of wild fruits, corn and oysters. In the ensuing days he explored what is now New York Harbor and sailed north on the river to the west of Manhattan island.

For eight days, Hudson explored this river which now bears his name. On either side were magnificent forests, beautiful hills, palisades and fertile valleys between, planted with Native American corn. The ship was moored at Kinderhook and the crew proceeded in smaller boats as far as the site of present-day Albany. It was a lovely river, but it was not the Northwest Passage.

On October 4, Hudson sailed for the Netherlands. En route back to Amsterdam, Hudson put in at Dartmouth on the south coast of England, where the ship was detained by orders of King James I and the crew claimed as Englishmen. Hudson was obliged to content himself with sending the Netherlands East India Company an account of his great discoveries and his enforced detention in England.

In fact, Hendrick Hudson was not greatly distressed by his captivity, and as it worked out English merchants furnished the money for another expedition. A ship called *Discovery* was given to Hudson, and in the summer of 1610, he again sailed for the West with a vision of the East Indies on his mind.

It had now been determined by a century of actual exploration that if the Northwest Passage existed, it did not exist between Florida and Maine. The whole coast had been minutely traced and no inlets found except bays and the estuaries of rivers. Therefore the coveted passage "must be" found far to the north, between the Gulf of St. Lawrence and Greenland.

was impossible to beat his way to the east through these inhospitable waters, he turned his prow to the west, determining if possible to find the Northwest Passage somewhere on the American coast.

It was in July, 1609, when Hudson sailed the *Half Moon* to the shores of Newfoundland. He sailed southward, touched Cape Cod, and by the middle of August arrived at Chesapeake Bay. Still the Northwest Passage was not to be found.

Turning to the north, Hudson examined the coast more closely than any of his predecessors. He entered and explored Delaware Bay and traced the coastline to New Jersey. By September, the *Half Moon* had reached Staten Island and had found a safe anchorage. Going ashore, Hudson was met by Native

Hudson now followed the path of Frobisher, and on August 2, he reached the strait now known as Hudson Strait. Frobisher had reached this point 32 years before, but no ship had ever before actually entered these waters. The entrance was barred with many islands, but further to the west the bay seemed to open, the ocean widened to right and left, and the route to China seemed to be at last revealed!

However, further to the west the inhospitable shores were seen to narrow again on the more inhospitable sea, and Hudson found himself surrounded with the terrors of winter in the frozen gulf of the north. He and his crew bore up against the hardships of his situation until their supplies were almost exhausted. Spring was almost at hand and the day of escape had well nigh arrived when the crew broke out in mutiny. They seized Hudson and his only son, along with seven others who had remained faithful to the commander, threw them into an open boat and cast them off among the icebergs. Nothing further was ever heard of the illustrious mariner who had contributed so largely to the geographical knowledge of his times and made possible the establishment of still another nationality in the New World.

Meanwhile, in 1610, the *Half Moon* had been liberated at Dartmouth and returned to Amsterdam, where the Dutch merchants were anxious to take advan-

*HENRY HUDSON'S SHIP, THE **HALF MOON**, ON THE HUDSON RIVER IN 1609.*

tage of the discoveries made by Hudson. If the Northwest Passage could not be found, they were ready to take advantage of the resources that actually did exist in this place.

Having failed to find gold in North America, France had turned to exploit the continent's vast population of beaver, and there were fortunes being made in the fur trade. The Dutch knew about this and decided to do the same.

Dutch ships were sent out to engage in the fur trade on the banks of the river that Hudson had discovered. This venture proved to be highly profitable, and in 1614, the States General of the Netherlands granted the Amsterdam merchants exclusive rights of trade within the limits of the area explored by Hendrick Hudson. Under this commission, five trading vessels soon arrived at Manhattan island, where some crude huts had already been built by former traders. A fort was built and the settlement was expanded and officially named New Amsterdam.

It was in 1626 that the Dutch, under Peiter Minuit (1580-1638), bought the entire Manhattan Island from the Canarsee Indian tribe for the reputed equivalent of $24, a transaction that is still cited as being the best real estate deal in American history, although the Dutch retained ownership of the island for only 38 years, and it would be three centuries before Manhattan's extraordinary importance would be realized.

Meanwhile, in the summer of 1614, Captain Adrian Block, commanding one of the Dutch trading ships, had made his way through the East River into Long Island Sound. He explored the coast as far as Narragansett Bay and Cape Cod, while Cornelius May, captain of the ship *Fortune*, sailed south along the coast as far as Delaware Bay. It was through these voyages, and the conquest of a tiny Swedish settlement on the Delaware River, that the Netherlands claimed the entire region as New Netherland.

It was to be a short-lived colonial experience. In 1664, the Dutch lost their colony to England, New Amsterdam was renamed New York in honor of the Duke of York, and the English became the dominant colonial power in eastern North America between Florida and the St. Lawrence. These colonies would form the basis for the original states of the United States.

NEW AMSTERDAM AS IT APPEARED AT THE TIME OF ITS 1664 TRANSFER TO THE ENGLISH.

WHERE TO GO

This section is designed as your guide to parks, historic sites, museums and interpretive centers in the United States and its territories where you can go to see what life was like in the historical period covered by *EXPLORATION & DISCOVERY*.

At these sites, you can see where many of the events in the book actually took place, or view exhibits relating to the everyday lives of the people, both Native and European, who lived and worked in North America in the period from 1492 to 1606 and beyond.

1. Natural History Museum of Los Angeles County
900 Exposition Boulevard
Los Angeles, CA 90007
(213) 748-6136

The history galleries in the museum depict life in California and the Southwest from 1540 to 1940, as well as United States history from the colonial period through 1914, and pre-Columbian archeology.

2. Old Town San Diego State Historic Park
Robinson-Rose House
4002 Wallace Street
San Diego, CA 92110
(619) 237-6770

Bordered by Wallace, Juan, Twiggs and Congress streets, this six block area commemorates the founding of the first permanent settlement in California by Gaspar de Portolá and a group of Spanish settlers in 1769.

3. Mission Basilica San Diego de Alcalá
10818 San Diego Mission Road
San Diego, CA 92108
(619) 281-8449

The mission is reached via I-80 to Mission Gorge Road and Twain Avenue. Founded by Father Junípero Serra on July 16, 1769 at Presidio Hill, the mission was the first of 21 California missions. It was moved to its present site in 1774, rebuilt in 1780 after an Indian attack, destroyed by earthquakes in 1803 and 1812 and fully restored in 1931.

4. Coronado National Memorial
4101 East Montezuma Canyon Road
Hereford, AZ 85615
(520) 366-5515/458-9333

Coronado National Memorial commemorates the first major exploration of the area by Europeans. The park lies on the United States-Mexican border within sight of the valley through which the Coronado Expedition first entered the present United States in search of the fabled Cities of Cíbola. Collections at the memorial include historical books, mid-16th century Spanish costumes, documents and weapons.

5. The Albuquerque Museum
2000 Mountain Road N.W.
Albuquerque, NM 87104
(505) 243-7255

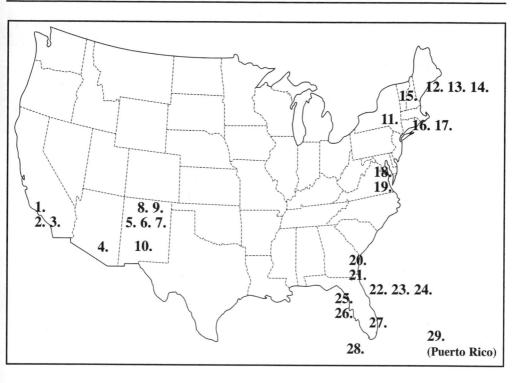

The central display features 400 years of Rio Grande Valley history. The museum provides a self-guiding tour brochure and a one hour guided walking tour of Old Town.

6. Spanish History Museum
2221 Lead Avenue S.E.
Albuquerque, NM 87106
(505) 268-9981

The museum displays drawings, photographs, coats of arms and memorabilia that illustrate Spain's influence on the American Southwest.

7. Acoma Pueblo (Sky City)
P.O. Box 309
Acoma, NM 87034
(800) 747-0181

Located near the junction of NM 23 and NM 32 about 60 miles west of Albuquerque, Acoma is the oldest continuously inhabited city in the United States, with many of its buildings appearing as they did when Coronado visited the site in the sixteenth century. Guided tours of this mesa-top city occur daily with the exception July 10-13 and one weekend in October. It is good to call ahead and arrive early. The view from the mesa is breathtaking.

8. Eight Northern Indian Pueblos
Eight Northern Indian Pueblos Council
P.O. Box 969
San Juan Pueblo, NM 87566
(505) 852 4265

The Eight Northern Indian Pueblos include the Nambe, Picuris, San Ildefonso, San Juan, Santa Clara, Taos and Tesque pueblos. Located in the Rio Grande Valley north of Santa Fe, New Mexico, they offer varying views of the life of Native Americans from the sixteenth century to the present. They are open to visitors throughout the year.

9. Palace of the Governors
National Historic Landmark
Palace Avenue
Santa Fe, NM 87501
(505) 827-6483

Constructed in 1610, the Palace of the Governors is the oldest seat of government in the United States. It is located on Santa Fe's central plaza at the end of the historic Santa Fe Trail. Now a museum, it offers exhibits relating to the history of the oldest European-established American city west of the Atlantic seaboard.

10. Salinas Pueblo Missions
National Monument
P.O. Box 496
Mountainair, NM 87036
(505) 847-2585

The Salinas Pueblo Missions National Monument is open daily, year around. The monument includes three sites: the Abó Ruins, nine miles west on US 60 and one half mile north on NM 513; the Gran Quivira Ruins, 26 miles south on NM 55; and the Quarai Ruins, eight miles north on NM 55 and one mile west. These sites feature church architecture, an unexcavated pueblo, excavated structures, museum exhibits, and a 40 minute film. The visitor center is in Mountainair, one block west of the US 60 and NM 55 junction.

11. New York Division of Tourism
One Commerce Plaza
Albany, NY 12245
(800) 225-56977

New York's Division of Tourism can provide information about seeing and visiting the homes and settlements of early Dutch settlers in the Hudson River Valley.

12. Acadia National Park
P.O. Box 177
Bar Harbor, ME 04609
(207) 288-3338

Comprised of ocean and mountain scenery, the park includes Mount Desert Island, discovered by Champlain in 1604, and the site of a short-lived French Jesuit settlement in 1613.

13. Maine Maritime Museum
263 Washington Street
Bath, ME 04530
(207) 443-1316

The focus of the 10 acre site is the maritime history of Maine since 1607, with an emphasis upon 19th century sailing ships. It includes two former shipyards; the restored Grand Banks schooner *Sherman Zwicker*; the Apprenticeshop, where traditional boat construction and repair skills are taught; and a collection of small craft used along Maine's coast and waterways. The museum also has a second site, the Sewell House, at 963 Washington Street, which features a large collection of marine paintings, sailor's artifacts and a children's room.

14. Colonial Pemaquid
State Historical Site
off SR 130
Pemaquid Point, ME 04558
(207) 677-2423

The museum displays artifacts excavated from the area and the site of an English settlement attempted in the early seventeenth century.

15. Heritage New Hampshire
1/2 mile north of US 302 on SR 16
Glen, NH 03838
(603) 383-9776

Uses audiovisual materials to trace 300 years of New Hampshire history, beginning with the voyage from England on a sailing ship and ending with a simulated train ride through Crawford Notch.

16. Ancient Burying Ground
60 Gold Street
Hartford, CT 06103
(203) 249-5631

This was Hartford's only cemetery until 1803. The oldest gravestone dates from 1636. The 1807 Center Church features six Tiffany windows. Tours are available by appointment only.

17. Old Stone Mill
Touro Park
Bellevue Avenue and Mill Street
Newport, RI 02840

Some believe that this stone mill was built by the Vikings long before Columbus arrived in the New World. Others think that the mill dates from the mid-seventeenth century.

18. The Smithsonian Institution
National Museum of American History
Constitution Avenue
Washington, DC 20560
(202) 357-2700

The Smithsonian includes numerous museums and galleries in the nation's capital. There are art galleries, museums, and research facilities. Of particular interest is the National Museum of American History on Constitution Avenue, which is perhaps the most complete and comprehensive collection anywhere of artifacts and and memorabilia relating to American history.

19. Colonial National Historical Park
Jamestown and Yorktown
P.O. Box 210
Yorktown, VA 23690
(804) 898-3400

Jamestown and Yorktown, located on the Virginia Peninsula, between the James and York rivers, are two eminent places in American history. Thanks to the Colonial Parkway it is easy to follow the sequence of history, from the colonial beginnings at Jamestown to the winning of national independence at York-town.

20. Fort King George
State Historic Site
P.O. Box 711
Darien, GA 31305
(912) 437-4770

Fort King George was the first British outpost in Georgia. From 1721 to 1736 it protected the Altamaha River and inner passage from French and Spanish attack.

21. Fort Caroline National Memorial
13 miles east of Jacksonville,
near the junction of Monument and Fort Caroline roads
Jacksonville, FL 32225
(904) 641-7155

Built in 1564 by French settlers led by René de Laudonnière, the settlers were routed and massacred the following year by the Spanish. The memorial covers 130 acres along the St. Johns River. A model of the original fort lies one quarter of a mile from the visitor's center. Ribault Monument, commemorating the first landing at St. Johns in 1562, lies one half mile east of the fort. Exhibits discuss the settlement in the context of the sixteenth century.

22. Castillo de San Marcos
National Monument
Castillo Drive, Avenida Menéndez
SR A1A and US 1
St. Augustine, FL 32084
(904) 829-6506

Castillo de San Marcos is the oldest masonry fort and the best preserved example of a Spanish colonial fortification in the continental United States. Exhibits trace the long history of the fort.

23. Fort Matanzas
National Monument
Visitor Information Center
10 Castillo Drive
St. Augustine, FL 32084
(904) 471-0116

The national monument includes the northern third of Rattlesnake Island and southern tip of Anastasia Island. A ferry carries visitors to Fort Matanzas, built from 1740 to 1742, located on Rattlesnake Island, off SR A1A, 14 miles south of St. Augustine. A visitor center is located on Anastasia Island, containing exhibits relating the fort's history.

24. Restored Spanish Quarter
Triay House
29 St. George Street
St. Augustine, FL 32084
(904) 825-6830

The area consists of restored and reconstructed buildings illustrating the Spanish colonial life. Guides in period costumes demonstrate 1740s crafts and lifestyles. Some of the buildings include: Casa de Gallegos (1750s), Casa de Gómez (1750s), DeHita/González houses and the Spanish Military Hospital.

25. De Soto National Memorial

P.O. Box 15390
Bradenton, FL 34280-5390
(813) 792-0458

The park is reached by taking State Route 64 west for approximately five miles from downtown Bradenton. Turn north (right) on 75th Street West and follow 2 1/2 miles to the park. A 22 minute film on the de Soto story is shown hourly. Artifacts of the de Soto period are on display in the small museum. Camp Ucita, a model encampment, represents the Native American village captured by de Soto for use as his first base camp.

26. Fort Myers Historical Museum

2300 Peck Street
Fort Myers, FL 33901
(813) 332-5955

Located in a restored railroad depot, the museum uses artifacts to depict the history of Fort Meyers and southwest Florida. Its focus is upon the Calusa and Seminole Indians, Spanish exploration and early settlers. Also on display is *The Esperanza*, the longest and last built Pullman private railroad car.

27. Dry Tortugas National Park
Everglades National Park

40001 SR 9336
Homestead, FL 33034
(305) 242-7700

The park is made up of the seven Tortugas Keys, or Dry Tortugas Islands, and the surrounding waters of the Gulf of Mexico. Discovered by Ponce de Léon in 1513, the Dry Tortugas are 68 nautical miles west of Key West. The islands, although they had no fresh water, were inhabited by pirates for centuries, preying upon the Spanish treasure ships as they passed the rocky islands. The Tortugas attract many migratory birds, including the sooty tern, and sea turtles. The remains of Fort Jefferson, begun in 1846, are located on Garden Key. The islands are accessible only by seaplane.

28. Maritime Museum
of the Florida Keys

102670 US 1
Key Largo, FL 33037
(305) 451-6444

Located on US 1 at Mile Marker 102, across from John Pennekamp Coral Reef State Park, the museum exhibits articles recovered from sunken ships dating back to the 17th century, as well as a reconstruction of a shipwreck site.

29. San Juan National Historic Site

Box 712
Old San Juan, Puerto Rico 00902

The San Juan National Historic Site includes the Spanish-built forts of El Morro, San Cristóbal, El Cañuelo and the city walls. The governor's palace, La Fortaleza, was erected as a fortress in the 1530s and is the oldest executive mansion in the Western Hemisphere still in use.

INDEX